BUT *WE* LOVE YOU, CHARLIE BROWN

Titan Facsimile Editions by Charles M. Schulz

On sale now:
Peanuts
More Peanuts
Good Ol' Charlie Brown
Good Grief, more Charlie Brown
Snoopy
You're Out of your Mind, Charlie Brown
Peanuts Revisited

Coming soon:
Go Fly a Kite, Charlie Brown
Peanuts Every Sunday

BUT *WE* LOVE YOU, CHARLIE BROWN

A NEW PEANUTS BOOK

By CHARLES M. SCHULZ

TITAN COMICS

BUT WE LOVE YOU, CHARLIE BROWN
ISBN: 9781782761617
PUBLISHED BY TITAN COMICS, A DIVISION OF TITAN PUBLISHING GROUP LTD,
144 SOUTHWARK ST, LONDON SE1 0UP. TCN 306.
© 2015 BY PEANUTS WORLDWIDE LLC.
PRINTED IN INDIA.

10 9 8 7 6 5 4 3 2 1

WWW.TITAN-COMICS.COM
WWW.PEANUTS.COM

ORIGINALLY PUBLISHED IN 1959 BY RHINEHART & CO. INCORPORATED
NEW YORK & TORONTO

A CIP CATALOGUE RECORD FOR THIS TITLE
IS AVAILABLE FROM THE BRITISH LIBRARY.
THIS EDITION FIRST PUBLISHED: NOVEMBER 2015

THROW ONE... GET BACK FIVE...

ALWAYS GIVE THE CLIENT MORE THAN HE ASKS FOR!

I AM A VERY PLEASANT PERSON... I ALWAYS TRY TO HAVE A KIND WORD FOR EVERYONE..

OH...

HI, CHARLIE BROWN...WHERE ARE YOU GOING?

I'M GOING TO GET A HAIRCUT...

WELL.... HAVE A NICE HAIRCUT!